Academic Writing

UNI SLOVAKIA series
Volume 3

Academic Writing

Selected Topics in Writing an Academic Paper

Silvia Gáliková

PETER LANG
EDITION

Bibliographic Information published by the Deutsche Nationalbibliothek

The Deutsche Nationalbibliothek lists this publication in the Deutsche Nationalbibliografie; detailed bibliographic data is available in the internet at http://dnb.d-nb.de

The publication of this book is part of the project Support for Improving the Quality of Trnava University (ITMS code 26110230092) — preparation of a Liberal Arts study program, which was supported by the European Union via its European Social Fund and by the Slovak Ministry of Education within the Operating Program Education. The text was prepared at the Department of Philosophy, Faculty of Philosophy, Trnava University in Trnava.

Design and Layout: © Jana Sapáková, Layout JS.
Printing: VEDA, Publishing House of the Slovak Academy of Sciences

ISBN 978-3-631-67340-9
E-ISBN 978-3-653-06588-6
DOI 10.3726/978-3-653-06588-6
ISSN 2366-2697

© Peter Lang GmbH
Internationaler Verlag der Wissenschaften
Frankfurt am Main 2016

Contents

Introduction 7

I.   The Mind and language 9

II.   Thinking and writing 19

III. Rhetoric and writing 29

IV.   Writing an essay 39

V.   The Structure of an essay 51

VI.   Logic in thoughts and words 61

VII. Logical fallacies 71

VIII. Cognitive biases 83

Bibliography 93

The heart has its reasons which reason knows nothing of.
Blaise Pascal

What can be said at all can be said clearly; and what we cannot talk about we must pass over in silence.
Ludwig Wittgenstein

Introduction

The aim of this text is to introduce students to a variety of factors that contribute to strong, well-organised writing. The following text will concentrate on selected topics and problematic aspects in preparing a cohesive and well-organised academic paper, such as: the relation between thinking and writing, establishing arguments and using logic and appropriate language in argumentative writing. In the following chapters the subject matter of philosophy is understood in presenting relevant arguments. Thus, the primary focus of a philosophy paper is the argument. An argument in philosophy is not merely a disagreement between people. An argument is a set of premises or reasons that are presented as support or grounds for believing a conclusion. If a claim is true, then there must be some good reasons for believing it.

The goal of a good argument is to present and defend true conclusions.

Philosophy is devoted to uncovering and clarifying the reasons that support conclusions and separating them from the claims that allegedly support the conclusion but fail. In philosophy papers we present, explain, and critically evaluate arguments. In some cases, a famous and influential argument will be the subject of a paper assignment. Sometimes a philosophy paper assignment will require a presentation and explanation of two or more arguments. Some philosophy paper assignments will ask you to present your own argument for your own conclusion about a given subject. Before the writing itself it is necessary to get ready for acquiring writing as a process, not a product.

Consider writing then as thinking made visible, as thinking in slow motion, a process whereby we can inspect and reflect on what we are thinking about. Writing doesn't simply convey thought, it also forges it. It is a two-way street, both expressing and generating ideas.

January 2015 S. G.

1 The Mind and language

Keywords: innateness, learning, language of thought, private language

Language use is a remarkable fact about human beings. The role of language as a vehicle of thought enables human thinking to be complex and varied. With language, one can describe the past or speculate about the future and so deliberate and plan in light of one's beliefs about how things stand. Language enables one to imagine counterfactual objects, events, and states of affairs. In this connection, it is intimately related to intentionality, the feature of all human thoughts whereby they are essentially about, or directed toward, things outside themselves. Language allows one to share information and to communicate beliefs and desires, attitudes and emotions. Indeed, it creates the human social world, rooting people into a common history and a common life experience. Language is equally an instrument of understanding and knowledge; the specialised languages of mathematics and science, for example, enable human beings to construct theories and make predictions about matters they would otherwise be completely unable to grasp. Language, in short, makes it possible for individual human beings to escape cognitive imprisonment in the here and now.

The evidently close connection between language and thought does not imply that there can be no thought without language. Although some philosophers and linguists have embraced this view, most regard it as implausible. Prelinguistic infants and at least the higher primates, for example, can solve quite complex problems, such as those involving spatial memory. This indicates real thinking, and it suggests the use of systems of representation – "maps" or "models" of the world— encoded in non-linguistic form. Similarly, among human adults, artistic or musical thought does not demand specifically linguistic expression: it may be purely visual or auditory. A more reasonable hypothesis regarding the connection between language and thought, therefore, might be the following: first, all thought requires representation of one kind or another; second, whatever the powers of non-linguistic representation that human adults may share with human infants and some other animals, those powers are immensely increased by the use of language. The powers and abilities conferred by the use of language entail cognitive successes of various kinds. But language may also be a source of cognitive failures. The idea that language is potentially misleading is familiar from many practical contexts. The same danger exists everywhere, however, including in scholarly and scientific research. In scriptural interpretation, for example, it is imperative to distinguish the true interpretations of a text from false ones; this in turn requires thinking about the stability of linguistic meaning and about the use of analogy, metaphor, and allegory in textual analysis. Often the danger is less that meanings may be misidentified, than that the text may be misconceived through alien categories entrenched in the scholar's own language.

The same worries apply to the interpretation of works of literature, legal documents, and scientific treatises. The "mist and veil of words" as the Irish philosopher G. Berkeley (1685–1753) described it, is a traditional theme in the history of philosophy. Confucius (551–479 bc), for example, held that, when words go wrong, there is no limit to what else may go wrong with them, for this reason, "the civilized person is anything but casual in what he says". This view is often associated with pessimism about the usefulness of natural language as a tool for acquiring and formulating knowledge. It has also inspired efforts by some philosophers and linguists to construct an "ideal" language – one that would be semantically or logically "transparent". The most celebrated of these projects was undertaken by the great German polymath, G. W. Leibniz (1646–1716), who envisioned a "universal characteristic" that would enable people to settle their disputes through a process of pure calculation, analogous to the factoring of numbers. In the early 20th century the rapid development of modern mathematical logic similarly inspired the idea of a language in which grammatical form would be a sure guide to meaning, so that the inferences that could legitimately be drawn from propositions would be clearly visible on their surface. Outside philosophy there have often been calls for replacing specialised professional idioms with ordinary language, which is always presumed to be free of obscurity and therefore immune to abuse.

What about the language we speak to ourselves, from the inside? In the philosophy of the mind a great discussion has originated from the so called "private language argument" an idea rejecting the existence of an "inner language" formulated by Ludwig Wittgenstein in his book, *Philosophical Investigations* (1953, §243): "The words of this language are to refer to what can be known only to the speaker; to his immediate, private, sensations. So another cannot understand the language". This is not intended to cover cases of recording one's experiences in a personal code, for such a code, however obscure in fact, could in principle be deciphered. What Wittgenstein had in mind is a language conceived as *necessarily* comprehensible only to its single originator because that which defines its vocabulary would be necessarily inaccessible to others. Immediately after introducing the idea, Wittgenstein goes on to argue that there cannot be such a language. The importance of drawing philosophers' attentions to a largely unheard-of notion and then arguing that it is unrealisable lies in the fact that an unformulated reliance on the possibility of a private language has been arguably essential to mainstream epistemology, the philosophy of the mind, and metaphysics, from Descartes to versions of the representational theory of the mind which became prominent in late 20th century cognitive science.

Some of the major issues at the intersection of philosophy of language and the philosophy of the mind are also dealt with in psycholinguistics. Scholars raise such important questions as, for example, how much of language is innate? Is language acquisition a special faculty in the mind? What is the connection between thought and language? There are at least three general perspectives on the issue of language learning.

The first is the behaviourist perspective, which dictates that not only is the solid bulk of language learned, but it is learned via conditioning. The second is the *hypothesis testing* perspective, which understands a child's learning of syntactic rules and meanings to involve the postulation and testing of hypotheses, through the use of the general faculty of intelligence. The final candidate for explanation is the innatist perspective, which states that at least some of the syntactic settings are innate and hardwired, based on certain modules of the mind. Cognitive scientists use heterogeneous notions of the structure of the brain when it comes to language. Connectionist models emphasise the idea that a person's lexicon and their thoughts operate in a kind of distributed, associative network. Nativist models assert that there are specialised devices in the brain that are dedicated to language acquisition. Computation models emphasise the notion of a representational language of thought and the logic-like, computational processing that the mind performs over them. Emergentist models focus on the notion that natural faculties are complex systems that emerge from simpler biological parts. Reductionist models attempt to explain higher-level mental processes in terms of the basic low-level neurophysiological activity of the brain.

An important problem for both the philosophy of language and the philosophy of the mind is, to what extent language influences thought and vice-versa. There have been a number of different perspectives on this issue, each offering a number of insights and suggestions. The linguists E. Sapir and B. Whorf suggested that language limits the extent to which members of a "linguistic community" can think about certain subjects and/or language was analytically prior to thought. The philosopher, M. Dummett, is also a proponent of the "language-first" viewpoint. In stark opposition to the Sapir–Whorf position is the notion that thought has priority over language. The "knowledge-first" position can be found in the work of P. Grice or J. Fodor in his language of thought hypothesis. According to this argument, spoken and written language derives their intentionality and meaning from an internal language encoded in the mind.

The language of thought hypothesis (LOTH) is an empirical thesis about the nature of thought and thinking. According to LOTH, thought and thinking are done in a mental language – in a symbolic system physically realised in the brain of organisms. In formulating LOTH, philosophers have in mind primarily the variety of thoughts known as "propositional attitudes". Propositional attitudes are thoughts described by such sentence forms as "S believes that P" "S hopes that P" "S desires that P" etc., where "S" refers to the subject of the attitude, "P" is any sentence, and "that P" refers to the proposition that is the object of the attitude. The main argument of this view is that the structure of thoughts and the structure of language seem to share a compositional, systematic character.

Another argument is that it is difficult to explain how signs and symbols on paper can represent anything meaningful unless some sort of meaning is infused into them by the contents of the mind. One of the main arguments against this stance is that such levels of language can lead to an infinite regress. Many philosophers of the mind and language, such as R. Millikan, F. Dretske and J. Fodor, have recently turned their attention to explaining the meanings of mental contents and states directly. Another tradition of philosophers has attempted to show that language and thought are coextensive – that there is no way of explaining one without the other (Davidson, Dennett). According to, for example, an externalist approach, the contents of at least some of one's mental states are dependent in part on their relationship to the external world or one's environment. Externalism is now a broad collection of philosophical views considering all aspects of mental content and activity (Quine, Putnam, Rorty).

Recent studies of the relationship between thought and language have been greatly inspired by the work of the cognitive linguists, G. Lakoff and M. Johnson. In their book, *Philosophy in the flesh* (1999), they argue in favour of a much stronger connection between thoughts and words than scholars have previously claimed. According to Lakoff and Johnson, the mind is embodied and its workings are strongly intertwined with the bodies (sensorimotor experience) and neuronal activity of the brain. Conceptual systems and our capacity for thought are thus shaped by the nature of our brains, bodies, and bodily interactions. Internally *felt* ideas and concepts expressed in language refer to things in the external (physical) world.

Suggested readings:

Fodor, J.: *The Modularity of Mind: An Essay on Faculty Psychology*. Cambridge: MIT Press, 1983.

Lakoff, G., Johnson, M.: *Philosophy in the Flesh*. New York: Basic Books, 1999.

Whorf, B., John B. Carroll (ed.): *Language, Thought, and Reality: Selected Writings of Benjamin Lee Whorf*. Cambridge: MIT Press, 1956.

II Thinking and writing

Keywords: thoughts, words, language, brainstorming, style

Words convey thoughts. Many scholars agree that in order to write well we need to think clearly. Similarly, the evidence is strong for concluding that writing about ideas can help to clarify them. Many would also argue that the act of writing can create ideas and lead writers to discover what they truly think. Language, according to this perspective, can give birth to thought, and written language provides a means of refining our thoughts since, unlike speech, written language can be manipulated until it accurately reflects our thinking. Many famous novelists and scientists have considered writing as a special challenge of reasoning on paper (E.M. Forster, I. Asimov, and Ch. Darwin). In their own special way they have stated the difficulty of expressing one's ideas on paper. I am sure that many of us, students and even more experienced writers, feel the same. As long as we use writing for describing events or fact, it seems easy, but where reasoning comes into play, to make a proper connection, a clearness and a moderate fluency, difficulties arise.

Although writing and thinking may be difficult, mastery and success in both can be well worth the effort. Clear writing is often essential. If we are not able to articulate a request, a complaint, or an endorsement in precise, forceful language, we will usually face problems in our everyday life. If we can't write a persuasive application, the job or graduate school position may go to someone else. If there is a strong relationship between thinking clearly and writing well, if one skill strengthens the other, then integrating the two as a course of study makes sense. But what does it mean to "think clearly". This term has achieved a central position in both contemporary academic and public life, and is variously defined. In most contexts, the term "critical" means censorious or faultfinding, but it comes to us from the Greek *kriticos* and Latin *criticus*, meaning able to discern or separate. It is the latter sense of critical that we will analyse; discriminate thought characterised by careful analysis and judgment.

The aim of the following text is therefore to emphasise the importance of an open mind and the element of self-defense implicit in critical thinking. The act of writing a paper involves several distinct tasks, such as: generating ideas, conducting research, focusing on a topic, establishing a thesis, organising the essay, organising paragraphs, providing transitions between sentences and paragraphs, choosing appropriate diction, polishing sentences for fluency, correcting grammar, usage, spelling, punctuation, etc. Each of these tasks could, of course, be broken down further.

At first sight it looks as though writing forces on us extremely complex objectives. In order to proceed in a disciplined manner, writing must be done in stages. It is a process that breaks down into roughly three stages: creating, shaping, and correcting. A common error students make is to focus their energies first on what should be the last stage (correcting), when their initial focus should be on the creative stage of the writing process. The effect of this misplaced attention is to inhibit creative thinking. It is essential that the writer gives enough time to the first stage, to generating ideas, to following impulsive thoughts even if they may initially appear unrelated or irrelevant. At this stage a writer must allow himself/herself to experience confusion, to be comfortable with chaos. He/she must learn to trust the writing process, to realise that in order to overcome chaos a logical train of thought will gradually emerge. Most important of all, writers must learn to suspend all criticism as they explore their topic and thinking.

Useful strategies for inventing and generating ideas are, for example, brainstorming and freewriting. To brainstorm, simply note the topic of the writing assignment at the top of a blank piece of paper or your computer screen. Then jot down words or phrases that come to mind as you think about this topic, as many words as possible, even if you are not sure they relate directly. After brainstorming, look at your list: circle the ideas that you want to develop, draw lines through those that are decidedly unrelated or uninteresting, and draw arrows or make lists of ideas that are connected to others. At this point you should be able to move on to the next stage: organising your essay either by writing an outline or by simply listing the main points that you want to develop into paragraphs. Brainstorming is particularly effective with two or more people. In free-writing, you begin by writing your topic on a blank sheet, but instead of jotting down words and phrases, you write continuously, using sentences that do not have have to be mechanically correct or connected. After freewriting for five to ten minutes, read over your text, circling the ideas you find interesting or insightful. At this stage you may engage in another freewriting on the idea, or ideas, you circled; or try to formulate a list of ideas you want to develop. One of the most often underestimated facts when writing an academic essay is closely related to the use of appropriate language. Standard requirements exist in choosing a relevant form of language that have to be respected. In writing an academic paper a student can implement more levels of formality.

The level of formality in writing should be determined by the expectations of your audience and your purpose. For example, if you are writing a cover letter for a job application or a college academic essay, you would write in a formal style. If you are writing a letter to a friend, writing something personal, or even writing something for a humourous magazine, when informal writing is expected, you would use a more informal style. A *formal* style should be used in the case of writing a text for an unknown audience (for example, applying for a job position advertised in the local paper). A *semi-formal* style should be used in a text written to a well-known individual. It is worth remembering that using an *informal* style is not only inappropriate, but simply incorrect (Hi! I read in the paper that ya'll were looking for a receptionist. I think that I'm good for this job because I've done stuff like it in the past, I'm good with words, and incredibly well organised).

As far as the proper use of language in an academic paper is concerned, it is important to avoid so-called group jargon: The term "jargon" refers to any in-group or specialised language used by small groups of like-minded individuals. This terminology is usually specialised to the function of the group, and will be used by and among group members as a sign of belonging, status, and for excluding outsiders. For example, individuals who study philosophy will use words like *Dasein, ontology, being, subject, epistemological, etc.* To non-philosophers, these words have different meanings or no meanings at all. Therefore, when making the choice of what vocabulary to use, it is important first and foremost to consider the audience you will be addressing. If you are writing for a general audience you should avoid using in-group jargon without explanations. Overloading your audience with words that they do not understand will not help you achieve your purpose. For example, if you are writing a paper explaining the concepts of philosophy to an audience of non-philosophers, you might introduce and explain a few important terms. But you should not use those terms without an explanation or in a way your audience cannot understand. If, however, you are writing to an in-group audience you will want to use group-specific jargon. Not using jargon when your audience expects it can signal to the audience that you are not a member of that group, or you have not mastered the group's terminology. This can damage your credibility and interfere with your purpose in writing. For example, if you are writing a conference paper for a group of philosophers, or a term paper for a college-level philosophy course, you should use in-group jargon to demonstrate that you understand the concepts and can discuss them in ways that other philosophers can.

Another danger a writer should be aware of is closely connected with the use of deceitful language and euphemisms. *Euphemisms* are terms that attempt to cover up that which is wrong, unethical, taboo, or harsh (for example, friendly fire = being shot at (unintentionally) by your own allies. Language can also be deceitful if it is overly complex or confusing. Confusing language is often deliberately complex and is used to downplay the truth or to evade responsibility. Finally, depending on the author's purpose, some terms that may be considered euphemisms can be appropriate or even sanctioned by the groups they affect. For example, it is more correct to say "persons with disabilities" or "differently-abled persons" than to call someone "handicapped" or even "disabled". In these cases, it is important to use what is considered correct by the group in question. Avoid using language that is stereotypical or biased in any way. Biased language frequently occurs with gender, but can also offend groups of people based on sexual orientation, ethnicity, political interest, or race (for example, "blacks" "slant-eyed"). The most important thing is to keep your writing clear and concise and make sure that you get your ideas across in a comprehensible form. This can be achieved through a well prepared, structured and organised draft.

Here are a few general points to remember when you are writing your assignments. As well as using appropriate language and aiming for 100 % accuracy in your grammar and vocabulary, you should also remember that you are writing for someone else, and hence the importance of punctuation, sentences, paragraphs and overall structure, all of which help the reader. What to avoid: a) too much personal language, b) emotive language (be objective rather than subjective), c) being too dogmatic (making sweeping generalisations), and d) sexist language. It is usually best to consistently use evidence from your source reading to back up what you are saying and reference it correctly. Check every word to make sure that it is providing something important and unique to a sentence. If words are dead weight, they can be deleted or replaced. Often writers use several small and ambiguous words to express a concept, wasting energy expressing ideas better relayed through fewer, specific words. As a general rule, more specific words lead to more concise writing. Because of the variety of nouns, verbs, and adjectives, most things have a closely corresponding description. Examples below actually convey more as they drop in word count:

Wordy: Suzie believed, but could not confirm, that Billy had feelings of affection for her (14 words).
Concise: Suzie assumed that Billy adored her (6 words).
Wordy: Our Web site has made available many of the things you can use to make a decision on the best dentist (20 words).
Concise: Our website presents criteria for determining the best dentist (9 words).
Wordy: The teacher demonstrated some of the various ways and methods for cutting words from my essay that I had written for class (22 words).
Concise: The teacher demonstrated methods for cutting words from my essay (10 words).

Also, do not forget to eliminate words that explain the obvious or provide excessive detail, for example: "René Descartes has been considered one of the most influential rationalist philosophers" "The atmosphere on Earth has the tendency of global overheating" etc. It is always important to consider your readers when drafting and revising your writing. Do not forget that one of the main objectives of your "written thoughts" consists in creating understanding in your readers' mind:

> We speak of understanding a sentence in the sense in which it can be replaced by another that says the same; but also in the sense in which it cannot be replaced by any other (Any more than one musical theme can be replaced by another). In the one case the thought in the sentence is common to different sentences; in the other, something that is expressed only by these words in these positions (Wittgenstein, 1953, §531).

Suggested readings:

Martinich, A. P.: *Philosophical Writing: An Introduction*. Oxford: Blackwell Publishing, 2005.

Murray, D. M.: Teach Writing as a Process Not Product. In: Villanueva, V. (ed.): *Cross-Talk in Comp Theory: A Reader*. Urbana: NCTE 2003, 3–6.

Wittgenstein, L.: *Philosophical Investigations*. Oxford: Blackwell, 1953.

III Rhetoric and writing

Keywords: ethos, pathos, logos, author, audience

As already stated in previous chapters, thoughts, spoken and written language are closely intertwined. In order to present a well-organised written work, scholars recommend analysing *rhetorical situations* – this term refers to any set of circumstances that involves at least one person using some sort of communication to modify the perspective of at least one other person. First of all, it is necessary to explain the meaning of the word "rhetoric". In brief, "rhetoric" is any communication used to modify the perspectives of others. Furthermore, knowledge and the use of rhetoric can help in understanding how people write more convincingly.

The ancient Greek philosopher, Aristotle, strongly influenced how people have traditionally viewed rhetoric. Aristotle defined rhetoric as "an ability, in each particular case, to see the available means of persuasion"

(Aristotle *Rhetoric* I.1.2). Aristotle's definition of rhetoric has been reduced in many situations to mean simply "persuasion". This approach to rhetoric has led to a long tradition of people associating rhetoric with politicians, lawyers, or other occupations noted for persuasive speaking. However, over the last century, the academic definition and use of "rhetoric" has evolved to include any situation in which people consciously communicate with each other. Individual people tend to perceive and understand just about everything differently from one another. This expanded perception has led a number of more contemporary rhetorical philosophers to suggest that rhetoric deals with more than just persuasion. Instead of just persuasion, rhetoric is the set of methods people use to *identify* with each other — to encourage each other to understand things from one another's perspectives.

From interpersonal relationships to international peace treaties, the capacity to understand or modify another's perspective is one of the most vital abilities that humans possess. Understanding rhetoric in terms of "identification" helps us to better communicate and evaluate all such situations. All human efforts to communicate occur within *innumerable* individual rhetorical situations that are particular to those specific moments of communication. An awareness of rhetorical situations can help in both composition and analysis. Each individual rhetorical situation shares five basic elements with all other rhetorical situations: a) text (the actual instance or piece of communication), b) author (someone who uses communication), c) audience (a recipient of communication), d) purposes (the varied reasons both authors and audiences have to communicate), and e) setting (the time, place, and environment surrounding a moment of communication). These five terms are updated versions of similar terms that Aristotle articulated over 2000 years ago. In his work on rhetoric, Aristotle analysed fundamental terms, such as: *logos*, *ethos*, and *pathos*, along with *kairos* and *telos*. Aristotle used these concepts to help explain how rhetoric functions.

Logos is frequently translated as some variation of "logic or reasoning", but it originally referred to the actual content of speech and how it was organised. Today, many people may discuss the *logos* qualities of a text to refer to how strong the logic or reasoning of the text is. But *logos* more closely refers to the structure and content of the text itself. *Ethos* is frequently translated as some variation of "credibility or trustworthiness", but it originally referred to the elements of speech that reflected on the particular character of the speaker or the speech's author. Today, many people may discuss the *ethos* qualities of a text to refer to how well an author portrays himself/herself. But *ethos* more closely refers to an author's perspective more generally. *Pathos* has been translated as some variation of "emotional appeal", but it originally referred to the elements of speech that appealed to any of an audience's sensibilities. Today, many people may discuss the *pathos* qualities of a text to refer to how well an author appeals to an audience's emotions. *Pathos* as "emotion" is often contrasted with *logos* as "reason". But this is a limited understanding of both *pathos* and *logos*; *pathos* more closely refers to an audience's perspective more generally. *Telos* is the term Aristotle used to explain the particular purpose or attitude of speech. Not many people use this term today in reference to rhetorical situations; nonetheless, it is instructive to know that early rhetorical thinkers placed much emphasis on speakers having a clear *telos*. Audiences can also have purposes of their own that differ from the speaker's purpose. *Kairos* is a term that refers to the elements of speech that acknowledge and draw support from the particular setting, time, and place that the speech occurs. Though not as commonly known as *logos*, *ethos*, and *pathos*, the term *kairos* has begun to receive renewed attention among teachers of composition since the mid-1980s. Although *kairos* may be well known among writing instructors, the term "setting" more clearly identifies this concept for contemporary readers.

All of aforementioned terms such as text, author, audience, purpose, and setting affect each other. Also, all of these terms have specific qualities that affect the ways in which they interact with the other terms. The word *text* is probably the most fluid term in a rhetorical situation. Usually, the word text refers to a written or typed document. In terms of a rhetorical situation, however, text means any form of communication that humans create. Whenever humans engage in any act of communication, the text serves as the vehicle for communication. Three basic factors that affect the nature of each text are: the medium of the text, the tools used to create the text, and the tools used to decipher the text. Texts can appear in any kind of medium, or mechanism for communicating. The plural of medium in this sense is media. Various media affect the ways that authors and audiences communicate. Consider how these different types of media can affect how and what authors communicate to audiences in various rhetorical situations: hand-written, typed, computer-generated, audio, visual, spoken, verbal, non-verbal, graphic, pictorial, and tactile, with words or without words. Some varied specific examples of media could include a paper, a speech, a letter, an advertisement, a billboard, a presentation, a poster-board, a cartoon, a movie, a painting, a sculpture, an email, a Twitter tweet, a Facebook post, graffiti, a conversation, etc. Every text is made with *tools* that affect the structure and content of the text. Such tools could be physical tools that range from the very basic (the larynx, throat, teeth, lips, and tongue necessary for verbal communication) to the very complex (a laptop computer with graphic-manipulating software). These tools could also be more conceptual tools that range from the simple (implementing feedback from an instructor) to the more complicated (implementing different kinds of library and primary research). The tools of communication often determine the kinds of communication that can happen in any given rhetorical situation. Likewise, audiences have varied tools for reading, viewing, hearing, or otherwise appreciating various texts. These could be actual physical tools that can range from the very basic (like the eyes and reading glasses necessary to read) to the very complex (like a digital projector and screen to view a PowerPoint presentation). Other types of conceptual tools could range from the simple (childhood principles learned from parents) to the more complicated (a Master's degree in art). The tools that audiences have at their disposal affect the ways that they appreciate different texts.

Author is a term used to refer to anyone who uses communication. An author could be one person or many people. It could be someone who uses writing (in a book), speech (in a debate), visual elements (in a TV commercial), audio elements (in a radio broadcast), or even tactile elements (Braille) to communicate. Whatever authors create, authors are human beings whose particular activities are affected by their individual backgrounds. These can include age, gender, geographic location, ethnicity, cultural experience, religious experience, social standing, personal wealth, sexuality, political beliefs, parents, level of education, personal experience, and others. All of these are powerful influences on what an author assumes about the world, who their audience is, what and how they communicate, and the settings in which they communicate. Gender, ethnicity, cultural experience, sexuality, and wealth factors are especially important in analysing rhetorical situations today. Many professionals in education, business, government, and non-profit organisations are especially aware of these specific factors in people's lives.

Like the term author, the term audience is also a fairly loose term. *Audience* refers to any recipient of communication. Audiences can read, hear, see, or feel different kinds of communication through different kinds of media. Also, like authors, audiences are human beings whose particular activities are affected by their specific backgrounds. The same factors that affect an author's background also affect an audience's background. Most importantly, these factors affect how audiences receive different pieces of communication, what they assume about the author, and the context in which they hear, read, or otherwise appreciate what the author communicates. Authors and audiences both have a wide range of purposes for communicating. The importance of purpose in rhetorical situations cannot be overstated. It is the varied purposes of a rhetorical situation that determine how an author communicates a text and how audiences receive a text. Rhetorical situations rarely have only one purpose. Authors and audiences tend to bring their own purposes to a rhetorical situation, and these purposes may conflict or complement each other depending on the efforts of both. Authors' purposes tend to be almost exclusively active, if only because authors conscientiously create texts for specific audiences. But audiences' purposes may range from passive to more active purposes. The role of purposes in communicating determine the basic rationale behind other decisions both authors and audiences make (what to write or speak about, or whom to listen to, etc.). An author's purpose in communicating could be to instruct, persuade, inform, entertain, educate, startle, excite, sadden, enlighten, punish, console, or many, many others. Like authors, audiences have varied purposes for reading, listening, or otherwise appreciating pieces of communication. Audiences may seek to be instructed, persuaded, informed, entertained, educated, startled, excited, saddened, enlightened, punished, consoled, or many, many others. An author's and audience's purposes are only limited to what the author and audience wish to accomplish in their moments of communication. There are as many purposes for communicating as there are words to describe those purposes.

Summing up; all situations involving communication involve at least one of each of the following: a) a text in a particular medium, created with certain tools, b) an author with a specific background, c) an audience with an equally specific background, d) the purposes of both the author and audience, and e) a setting in a particular time and place involving a certain community and conversation. Understanding the factors that shape rhetorical situations make authors and audiences more aware of what goes into different acts of communication. Overall, understanding these factors helps people better understand the differing perspectives of others.

Suggested readings:

Aristotle: *On Rhetoric: A Theory of Civic Discourse*. 2nd ed. Trans. George A. Kennedy. New York: Oxford UP, 2007.

Burke, K.: *A Rhetoric of Motives*. Berkeley: University of California Press, 1969.

Richard, J., Paine, Ch.: *Writing Today*. New York: Pearson Education, 2010.

IV Writing an essay

Keywords: narrative, exposition, argumentation, clarity, assignment

The essay is a commonly assigned form of writing that every student will encounter while in academia. Essays can be a rewarding and challenging type of writing and are often assigned either to be done in class, which requires previous planning and practice on the part of the student, or as homework, which likewise demands a certain amount of preparation. Students can avoid the discomfort often associated with essay writing by understanding some common genres within essay writing.

What is an essay? Though the word *essay* has come to be understood as a type of writing in Modern English, its origins provide us with some useful insights. The word comes into the English language through the French influence on Middle English. Tracing it back further, we find that the French form of the word comes from the Latin verb *exigere*, which means "to examine, test, or to drive out". Essays are shorter pieces of writing that require the student to acquire a number of skills such as close reading, analysis, comparison and contrast, persuasion, conciseness, clarity, and exposition. The purpose of an essay is to encourage students to develop ideas and concepts in their writing with the direction of expanding on their own thoughts. Therefore, essays are concise and require clarity in purpose and direction; the writing must be deliberate and interesting. A variety of genres can be recognised in essay writing: a) expository, b) descriptive, c) narrative, and d) argumentative.

An *expository essay* is a genre of essay that requires the student to investigate an idea, evaluate evidence, expound on the idea, and set forth an argument concerning that idea in a clear and concise manner. This can be accomplished through comparison and contrast, definition, example, the analysis of cause and effect, etc. The structure of an expository essay is held together by a *clear, concise, and defined thesis statement* that occurs in the first paragraph of the essay. It is essential that this thesis statement be appropriately narrowed to follow the guidelines set forth in the assignment. The next principle is concerned with clear and logical transitions between the introduction, body, and conclusion. Transitions are the "building blocks" that hold the foundation of the essay together. Without a logical progression of thought, the reader is unable to follow the essay's argument, and the structure will collapse. Each paragraph should be limited to the exposition of one general idea. This will allow for clarity and direction throughout the essay. What is more, such conciseness creates an ease of readability for the audience. It is important to note that each paragraph in the body of the essay must have some logical connection to the thesis statement in the opening paragraph. The conclusion is the point of the essay that students often struggle with. This is the portion of the essay that will leave the most immediate impression on the mind of the reader. Therefore, it must be effective and logical. In summarising one's ideas, it is recommended not to introduce any new information but rather, to synthesise and come to a conclusion concerning the information already presented in the body of the essay.

A *descriptive essay* is a genre of essay that asks the student to describe something — an object, person, place, experience, emotion, situation, etc. This genre encourages the student's ability to create a written account of a particular experience. What is more, it allows for a great deal of artistic freedom. Guidelines for writing a descriptive essay mainly include: the use of clear and concise language, a careful use of words, and particularly their relevancy in relation to the described subject matter.

When writing a *narrative essay*, one might think of it as telling a story. These essays are often anecdotal, experiential, and personal allowing students to express themselves in creative and, quite often, moving ways. Writing an interesting narrative essay includes the following: in the case of writing a story, the essay should include all of the parts of a story – an introduction, plot, characters, setting, climax, and conclusion – the essay should have a purpose, and should be written from a clear point of view. It is quite common for narrative essays to be written from the standpoint of the author. Creativity in narrative essays often times manifests itself in the form of an authorial perspective. Much like the descriptive essay, narrative essays are effective when the language is carefully, particularly, and artfully chosen. In order to evoke specific emotions and senses in the reader, the use of the first person pronoun "I" is a must.

An *argumentative essay* is a genre of writing that requires the investigation of a topic, the collection, generation, and evaluation of evidence, and establishing a position on the topic in a concise manner. Some confusion may occur between the argumentative essay and the expository essay. These two genres are similar, but the argumentative essay differs from the expository essay in the amount of pre-writing and research involved. The argumentative essay is commonly assigned as a capstone or final project in first year writing or advanced composition courses, and involves lengthy, detailed research. Expository essays involve less research and are shorter in length. Argumentative essay assignments generally call for extensive research of literature or previously published material. Argumentative assignments may also require empirical research where the student collects data through interviews, surveys, observations, or experiments. Regardless of the amount or type of research involved, argumentative essays must establish a clear thesis and follow sound reasoning. The structure of an argumentative essay is held together by the following: a clear, concise, and defined thesis statement that occurs in the first paragraph of the essay. In the first paragraph of an argumentative essay, students should set the context by reviewing the topic in a general way. Next, the author should explain why the topic is important or why readers should care about the issue. Lastly, students should present their thesis statement. It is essential that the thesis statement be appropriately narrowed to follow the guidelines set forth in the assignment. If the student does not master this portion of the essay, it will be quite difficult to compose an effective or persuasive essay. Clear and logical transitions between the introduction, body, and conclusion are another fundamental requirement. Transitions are the "building blocks" that hold the foundation of the essay together. Without logical progression of thought, the reader is unable to follow the essay's argument, and the structure will collapse. Transitions should wrap up the idea from the previous section and introduce the idea that is to follow in the next section. Each paragraph should be limited to the discussion of one general idea. This will allow for clarity and direction throughout the essay. In addition, such conciseness creates an ease of readability for the audience. It is important to note that each paragraph in the body of the essay must have some logical connection to the thesis statement in the opening paragraph. Some paragraphs will directly support the thesis statement with evidence collected during research. It is also important to explain how and why the evidence supports the thesis. However, argumentative essays should also consider and explain differing points of view regarding the topic. Depending on the length of the assignment, students should dedicate one or two paragraphs of an argumentative essay to discussing conflicting opinions on the topic. Rather than explaining how these differing opinions are wrong outright, students should note how opinions that do not align with their thesis might not be well informed or how they might be out of date. An argumentative essay requires well-researched, accurate, detailed, and current information to support the thesis statement and consider other points of view. Some factual, logical, statistical, or anecdotal evidence could support the thesis.

As already stated in previous sections, the main objective of this textbook is to help in developing students' critical thinking skills, to help them acquire an understanding of important philosophical issues, and assist them in better presenting and evaluating arguments, thus resulting in better writing. In a philosophy paper, the argument(s) should be stated with as much clarity and precision as possible. The conclusions of the arguments and the premises should be stated simply and clearly. Every philosophy paper should contain a clearly articulated thesis. The *thesis* is the central or overall claim that you are arguing for. If the paper is expository, then your thesis will simply state the expository goal of the paper, "Aristotle endorses a virtue theory of morality" for instance, could be the thesis of an expository paper that asked you to present and explain Aristotle's theory of ethics. The thesis of an argumentative paper will clearly state the position that you are going to endorse in a philosophical debate. "I will argue that Aristotle's moral theory fails because it does not provide an adequate account of specific moral actions" is an example of an argumentative thesis for a paper assignment that asks you to present and critically evaluate Aristotle's moral theory. "The physicalist hypothesis is inadequate in studying consciousness" is another example of an argumentative thesis in a paper about the explanation of consciousness, and so on. However, students must consider multiple points of view when collecting evidence.

As noted in the paragraph above, a successful and well-rounded argumentative essay will also discuss opinions not aligning with the thesis. It would be unethical to exclude evidence that may not support the thesis. It is therefore important to point out how other positions may not be well informed or up to date on the topic. Even if you agree with the conclusion of an argument and you believe that the reasoning is sound, a good philosophy paper will address potential objections and defend against them. Rather than simply agreeing with the author, present some possible objections and either explain how the author would respond to them, or what potential responses are available. You might disagree with the conclusion and the premises given to support it. Your critical evaluation will be similar to the previous case, but you will also explain which conclusion you think is true and why. You are not being indoctrinated into a dogma. Rather, you are being evaluated on your critical thinking and writing abilities. What you conclude is often not as important as explaining how you arrived at those conclusions. What is important in your critical evaluation is that you raise some plausible and well-defended objections to the position that you presented earlier in the paper. Explain and defend the criticism you are presenting. Do not present open, unanswered, or rhetorical questions. "Who's to say what a just society is?" or "How does Hume know that there is no physical substance?" are examples of the worst kind of anti-intellectual comments. State the objection that is behind these questions and explain each step of the philosopher's arguments carefully and deliberately. New terms need to be explained and the inferences that the author makes from one step of the argument to the next should be clear. A common mistake of philosophy papers is the failure to explain important concepts and arguments.

When writing a paper a student can make claims falling into several categories, such as: claims of fact or definition, claims of cause and effect, claims about value, etc. Claims of fact or definition argue about what the definition of something is or whether something is a settled fact. Example: What some people refer to as global warming is actually nothing more than normal, long-term cycles of climate change. Philosophy papers often use claims of cause and effect to argue that one person, thing, or event caused another thing or event to occur. Example: A mental event such as a decision caused John to undertake more psychology classes. Claims about value consist of what something is worth, whether we value it or not, how we would rate or categorise something. Example: Global warming is the most pressing challenge facing the world today. What type of thesis or claim you use for your argument will depend on your position and knowledge of the topic, your audience, and the context of your paper. You might want to think about where you imagine your audience to be on this topic and pinpoint where you think the biggest difference in viewpoints might be. Even if you start with one type of claim you will probably be using several within the paper. Regardless of the type of claim one chooses to utilise it is key to identify the controversy or debate you are addressing and to define your position early on in the paper.

The question of using research and evidence in a philosophical-theoretical essay sometimes raises unnecessary confusions. It is always up to the writer to justify the use of evidence, whether it is experimental research, empirical findings, or conceptual models. First hand, or primary research, is research you have conducted yourself such as interviews, experiments, surveys, or personal experience and anecdotes. In spite of the theoretical character of most philosophy papers, writers use such types of evidence, not only to supplement, but also in support of their arguments and claims. Second hand, or secondary research, is research obtained from various texts that have been supplied and compiled by others, such as books or periodicals. Regardless of what type of sources you use, they must be credible. In other words, your sources must be reliable, accurate, and trustworthy. In order to determine if a source is credible, it is necessary to ask the following questions: Who is the author? Credible sources are written by authors respected in their fields of study. Responsible, credible authors will cite their sources so that you can check the accuracy of and support for what they have written. How recent is the source? The choice to seek recent sources depends, of course, on the topic of the essay. What is the author's purpose? When deciding which sources to use, you should take the purpose or point of view of the author into consideration. Is the author presenting a neutral, objective view of a topic? Or is the author advocating one specific view of a topic? Who is funding the research or writing of this source? A source written from a particular point of view may be credible; however, you need to be careful that your sources don't limit your coverage of a topic to one side of a debate. What type of sources does your audience value? If you are writing for a professional or academic audience, they may value peer-reviewed journals as the most credible sources of information. A younger audience may be more accepting of information found on the Internet than an older audience might be. When evaluating Internet sources, the writer has to be especially careful. Avoid using *Wikipedia* or other sites that are collaboratively developed by users. Because anyone can add or change content, the validity of information on such sites may not meet the standards for academic research.

Suggested readings:

Murray, D. M.: Teach Writing as a Process Not Product. In: Villanueva, V. (ed.): *Cross-Talk in Comp Theory: A Reader*. Urbana: NCTE 2003, 3–6.
Sternberg, R.J.: *Kognitivní psychologie*. Praha: Portál, 2002.

V The Structure of an essay

Keywords: exposition, critical evaluation, conclusion, paragraph, coherence

Most philosophy papers have the following structure: a) introduction, b) exposition, c) critical evaluation, and d) conclusion. *Introduction*: The introductory part of a paper should state the thesis that the paper will defend. Briefly outline the argument that will support the thesis, discuss the position being presented, or the issues that the paper will discuss, and state the plan for the paper. *Exposition*: In the exposition it is expected that the author will explain the argument regarding the topic stated in the introduction, and that all important attributions will be supported with quotes, paraphrases, and citations from the text(s). It is of great importance to make each step of the argument as clear as possible. *Critical Evaluation*: In argumentative papers, a sound critical evaluation plays a crucial role. It includes the enumeration of any problems with the arguments laid out in the text(s), explained and supported with textual references. *Conclusion:* Restate the thesis of the paper. Briefly restate the basic issues that were explained in every part of the paper, and the criticisms explained and defended.

The introduction of your paper should range from a few paragraphs, to a page or two, depending on the length of the paper. Avoid abstract or empty sentences like, "I will then describe the argument that Searle gives for his conclusion". A brief statement of the argument is much better and informs the reader about the subject of the paper: "Searle argues that computers cannot think because computers are incapable of intentionality and understanding". Similarly, "I will conclude that Kant's argument concerning space is mistaken because of developments in modern mathematics" is more illuminating to the reader than, "I will draw conclusions in this paper". Try not to intermingle separate parts of the text. While it may seem intuitive to criticise a point in an argument immediately after you have explained it, the reader is probably not clear at this point on the overall structure or goal of the argument. First, the whole argument has to be sufficiently explained before evaluating it. Many times students hand in a paper which has been written exclusively "for the teacher".

The conclusion should contain no surprises; therefore try to avoid bringing up new issues, new criticisms, or different comments that belonged in the exposition or critical evaluation section. Students also often make interesting suggestions about what is wrong with the philosopher's position in the last few sentences of the paper without spelling out the details. Such comments belong in the body of the paper. The conclusion should, for the most part, restate the central accomplishments of the paper.

In order to write a comprehensive and articulate essay, attention should be paid to *how* one "puts ideas on paper". Preliminary requirements include: consulting a standard manual of grammar and style for a complete listing of the rules of grammar, punctuation, usage and style. In order to prepare a sound draft of your future paper, you should also avoid frequently occurring writing problems. Common problems occur with the use of certain words and phrases such as "very" "really" and "basically" which are clumsy words to use in an academic paper. They do not add anything to a sentence that is not said without them. "Further" often has the same problem or is misused, "he further argues that" says little that, "he argues that" or "he then argues that" does not. The same goes for the use of vacuous or empty claims. Each sentence in your paper is an important opportunity to say something about the assigned topic. Sometimes we write sentences that on the surface seem to make a claim of substance, but nothing is actually stated. Consider what is said in this example, "From this point forward other issues that Descartes proclaims in the Meditations are expressed and are thoroughly reasoned". When we simplify this sentence it seems to be saying that Descartes expresses and reasons some issues. But this point doesn't need to be made. What is important for a philosophy paper is the content of those claims. A sentence about what specific claims Descartes makes, or how he reasons from one point to the next would be much better. Use transitions or write sentences so that the connection to the previous and next sentence is clear to your reader.

All paragraphs should have a clear thesis sentence that relates clearly to the thesis of the paper. Usually the thesis sentence is at the beginning of the paragraph where it can help the reader understand how the point being made fits into the purpose of the paper. The rest of the paragraph should support this thesis sentence with explanations, quotes, and citations from the text(s). If you are going to make a new point, then start a new paragraph. Be careful about jumping too quickly from one point to the next or mixing too many issues together. All new or different topics should be gathered together by theme and put into new paragraphs. Each paragraph should have a cohesive unity that resembles a well-written paper. Use transitions to make it clear to your reader how the paragraph is related to the previous or next paragraph. Connect your paragraphs in a logical way, even if that means saying in the first sentence of a paragraph something like "Having discussed X, I will now consider Y". "Now that we have seen what the faculty of the will is for Kant, the next issue that needs to be addressed is what conditions make a will good instead of bad" is an example of a transition sentence that clarifies the connection between the issues being discussed in the adjacent paragraph(s), and helps the reader see the development of points in the paper.

A topic that is often times underestimated concerns *writing style*. The diction of an academic essay should be more formal than conversational language. We all say things like, "I don't buy that argument" or "What does she say about that?" in conversation, but those kind of casual comments are not appropriate for the subject matter or context of a college paper. Another important issue relates to the use of clichés or generalisations in the writing. Phrases like, "For thousands of years, philosophers have wondered about" or "for all intents and purposes" or "everyone knows" are cheap sayings that indicate to the reader that the author does not choose his/her words carefully. Sayings like these get used so often that they lose their meaning.

A number of problems arise when using *quotes* and quoting. You should make use of relevant quotes to support any major attributions that you make regarding the author being discussed. If you claim, "Descartes believes that the mind is indivisible" for instance, you should provide a quote and citation of the passage where he makes that claim. Quotes not only need to be introduced, but at the same time explained: "Descartes claims" "Socrates states" or "Wittgenstein believes" etc. The relevance, implication, and meaning of the author's claims in a quote need to be explained immediately after or before the quote. The majority of the paper should be your own words, with support from the text(s). A persisting problem within any kind of academic paper is an inability to distinguish between a quote, a paraphrase, and one's own ideas. It is of immense importance to articulate clearly the analysed author's thoughts from the thoughts of others. In every case where someone else's work, ideas, research, or writing is used in your paper, a citation must be given providing appropriate credit. Citations should be given as footnotes, endnotes, or in another standard and approved format. Do not forget to use a standard format for citing your sources. Double check your spellings of proper names and philosophy terms that will not be in your spellchecker.

Check your paper carefully for grammar and punctuation mistakes. Some of the most common mistakes in college writing are commas, and apostrophes in contractions and possessives. I always recommend that students read their paper out loud or have someone else read it or proofread it. Reading your paper out loud will allow you or your reader to notice awkward phrases, run-on sentences, non-sequiturs, and other problems that you may not notice otherwise.

Each part of the essay consists of a number of paragraphs. What is a paragraph? A paragraph is a collection of related sentences dealing with a single topic. Learning to write good paragraphs forms the basic prerequisite for the writer. Even the most original ideas have to be presented in an organised fashion. Good paragraphing greatly assists readers in following a piece of writing. The basic rule of thumb with paragraphing is to keep one idea to one paragraph. In the case of a transition into a new idea, it is necessary to continue in a new paragraph. There are some simple ways to tell if you are on the same topic or a new one. You can have one idea and several bits of supporting evidence within a single paragraph. You can also have several points in a single paragraph as long as they relate to the overall topic of the paragraph. If the single points start to get long, then perhaps elaborating on each of them and placing them in their own paragraphs is the route to go. To be as effective as possible, a paragraph should contain each of the following: a) unity, b) coherence, c) a topic sentence, and d) adequate development. Using and adapting these overlapping traits will surely help in constructing effective paragraphs.

Unity: Achieving unity requires that the entire paragraph is concerned with a single focus. If the text begins with one focus or major point of discussion, it should not end with another or wander within different ideas. *Coherence* is the trait that makes the paragraph easily understandable to a reader. Tools that can help create coherence in paragraphs are called logical bridges and verbal bridges. *Logical bridges* are used when the same idea of a topic is carried over from sentence to sentence. Successive sentences can be constructed in parallel form. Within *verbal bridges,* keywords can be repeated in several sentences. Synonymous words can be repeated in several sentences, pronouns can refer to nouns in previous sentences. Also, transition words can be used to link ideas from different sentences. *A topic sentence* is a sentence that indicates in a general way what idea or thesis the paragraph is going to deal with. Although not all paragraphs have clear-cut topic sentences, and despite the fact that topic sentences can occur anywhere in the paragraph (as the first sentence, the last sentence, or in the middle), an easy way to make sure the reader understands the topic of the paragraph is to put a topic sentence near the beginning of the paragraph. Regardless of whether you include an explicit topic sentence or not, you should be able to easily summarise what the paragraph is about. *Adequate development* means that the topic should be discussed fully and adequately. Again, this varies from paragraph to paragraph, depending on the author's purpose, but writers should be wary of paragraphs that only have two or three sentences.

As stated above, a new paragraph starts when introducing a new idea or point. If you have an extended idea that spans multiple paragraphs, each new point within that idea should have its own paragraph. Separate paragraphs can serve to contrast sides in a debate, different points in an argument, or any other difference. Breaks between paragraphs function as a short "break" for readers, adding these in will help the writing to become more readable. An author creates a break usually if the paragraph becomes too long or the material is complex. Introductory and concluding material should always be in a new paragraph. Many introductions and conclusions have multiple paragraphs depending on their content, length, and the writer's purpose.

Two very important elements of paragraphing are signposts and transitions. Signposts are internal aids to assist readers; they usually consist of several sentences or a paragraph outlining what the article has covered and where the article will be going. Transitions are usually one or several sentences that "transition" from one idea to the next. Transitions can be used at the end of most paragraphs to help the paragraphs flow one into the next.

Suggested readings:

Johnson, Sh.R., Charles, P.: *Writing Today*. New York: Pearson Education, 2010.

Raimes, A.: *Pocket keys for writers*, 3rd Edition. New York: Wadsworth Cengage Learning, 2010.

Swales, J. M., C. B. Feak: *Academic writing for graduate students: Essential tasks and skills*, 2nd Edition. Ann Arbor: University of Michigan Press, 2009.

VI Logic in thoughts and words

Keywords: syllogism, argumentation, premise, induction, deduction

As repeatedly stated in the preceding section of this text, thinking and writing are mutually intertwined. According to the recognised American author and narrator, D. McCullough, "Writing is thinking. To write well is to think clearly. That's why it's so hard". And he seems to be absolutely right. So let's get back to the process of writing itself. The following text is designed to help students develop and use *logical* arguments in writing, analyse the arguments of others and generate their own arguments.

There are three types of persuasive strategies, used to support claims and respond to opposing arguments: 1) logos, 2) inductive reasoning, and 3) deductive reasoning. A good argument will generally use a combination of all three appeals to make its case. *Logos,* or the appeal to reason, relies on logic or reason. Logos often depends on the use of inductive or deductive reasoning.

Inductive reasoning takes a specific representative case or facts and then draws generalisations or conclusions from them. Inductive reasoning must be based on a sufficient amount of reliable evidence. In other words, the facts you draw on must fairly represent the larger situation or population. There are varying degrees of strength and weakness in inductive reasoning, and various types including statistical syllogism, arguments from example, causal inferences, simple inductions, and inductive generalisations. They can have part to whole relations, extrapolations, or predictions. Example: Every windstorm in this area comes from the north. I can see a big cloud of dust caused by a windstorm in the distance; so, a new windstorm is coming from the north. *Deductive reasoning* begins with a generalisation and then applies it to a specific case. The generalisation you start with must have been based on a sufficient amount of reliable evidence. Deductive reasoning is based on premises and if the premises are true, then the reasoning will be valid. In mathematics, if A = B and B = C, then A = C. Examples from everyday experience: All birds have feathers and robins are birds, so robins have feathers; Elephants have cells in their bodies and all cells have DNA, so elephants have DNA.

Some deductive reasoning does not follow the classic reasoning pattern of A = B and B = C, then A = C. Examples of other patterns are: Be careful around bees, they might sting you (The reasoning is understood that all bees might sting). The apple hit me on the head because of gravity.

To be logical, a proposition must be tested within a logical sequence. The Greek philosopher Aristotle developed the most famous logical sequence, called the syllogism. His most famous syllogism is:

Premise 1: All men are mortal.
Premise 2: Socrates is a man.
Conclusion: Therefore, Socrates is mortal.

In this sequence, premise 2 is tested against premise 1 to reach a logical conclusion. Within this system, if both premises are considered valid, there is no other logical conclusion than determining that Socrates is a mortal. Logical vocabulary includes the following concepts:

Premise: A proposition used as evidence in an argument.
Conclusion: The logical result of the relationship between the premises. Conclusions serve as the thesis of the argument.
Argument: The assertion of a conclusion based on logical premises.
Syllogism: The simplest sequence of logical premises and conclusions, devised by Aristotle.
Enthymeme: A shortened syllogism that omits the first premise, allowing the audience to fill it in. For example,

"Socrates is mortal because he is a human" is an enthymeme that leaves out the premise "All humans are mortal".

(*Induction*: A process through which the premises provide some basis for the conclusion.

Deduction: A process through which the premises provide conclusive proof for the conclusion.)

Reaching logical conclusions depends on the proper analysis of premises. The goal of a syllogism is to arrange premises so that only one true conclusion is possible. Consider the following premises:

Premise 1: Non-renewable resources do not exist in infinite supply.
Premise 2: Coal is a non-renewable resource.
From these two premises, only one logical conclusion is available:
Conclusion: Coal does not exist in infinite supply.

Often logic requires several premises to reach a conclusion.

Premise 1: All monkeys are primates.
Premise 2: All primates are mammals.
Premise 3: All mammals are vertebrate animals.
Conclusions: Monkeys are vertebrate animals.

Logic also allows specific conclusions to be drawn from general premises, for example:

Premise 1: All squares are rectangles.
Premise 2: Figure 1 is a square.
Conclusion: Figure 1 is also a rectangle.

Furthermore, logic requires decisive statements in order to work. Therefore, this syllogism is false:

Premise 1: Some quadrilaterals are squares.
Premise 2: Figure 1 is a quadrilateral.
Conclusion: Figure 1 is a square.

This syllogism is false because not enough information is provided to allow a verifiable conclusion. Figure 1 could just as likely be a rectangle, which is also a quadrilateral.

Logic can also mislead when it is based on premises that an audience does not accept. For instance:

Premise 1: People with red hair are not good at checkers.
Premise 2: Bill has red hair.
Conclusion: Bill is not good at checkers.

Within the syllogism, the conclusion is logically valid. However, it is only true if an audience accepts Premise 1, which is very unlikely. This is an example of how logical statements can appear accurate while being completely false.

Logical conclusions also depend on which factors are recognised and ignored by the premises. Therefore, different premises could lead to very different conclusions about the same subject. For instance, these two syllogisms about the platypus reveal the limits of logic for handling ambiguous cases:

A. Premise 1: All birds lay eggs.
Premise 2: Platypuses lay eggs.
Conclusion: Platypuses are birds.
B. Premise 1: All mammals have fur.
Premise 2: Platypuses have fur.
Conclusion: Platypuses are mammals.

Though logic is a very powerful argumentative tool and is far preferable to a disorganised argument, logic does have limitations. It must also be effectively developed from a syllogism into a written piece.

Logic is a very effective tool for persuading an audience about the accuracy of an argument. However, people are not always persuaded by logic. Sometimes audiences are not persuaded because they have used values or emotions instead of logic to reach conclusions. But just as often, the audience may have reached a different logical conclusion by using different premises. Therefore, arguments must often spend as much time convincing audiences of the legitimacy of the premises as the legitimacy of the conclusions.

It is important to remember that logic is only one aspect of a successful argument. *Non-logical* arguments, statements that cannot be logically proven or disproved, are also important in argumentative writing, such as appeals to emotions or values. *Illogical arguments*, on the other hand, are false and must be avoided. Logic is a formal system of analysis that helps writers invent, demonstrate, and prove arguments. It works by testing propositions against one another to determine their accuracy. People often think they are using logic when they avoid emotion or make arguments based on their common sense, such as "Everyone should look out for their own self interests" or "People have the right to be free". However, unemotional or common sense statements are not always equivalent to logical statements.

Thought experiments play a rather special place within philosophical argumentation. They are defined as devices of the imagination used to investigate the nature of things. Thought experiments are used for diverse reasons in a variety of areas, including economics, history, mathematics, philosophy, and the sciences – especially physics. Most often thought experiments are communicated in narrative form. Thought experiments should be distinguished from thinking about experiments, from merely imagining experiments to be conducted outside the imagination, and from psychological experiments with thoughts. They should also be distinguished from counterfactual reasoning in general, as they seem to require an experimental element, which seems to explain the impression that something is experienced in a thought experiment. In other words, though many call any counter-factual or hypothetical situation a thought experiment, this seems too encompassing. Here are some frequently used thought experiments used in philosophical argumentation.

The first experiment, called *Mary the colourblind neuroscientist,* sometimes refers to the *knowledge argument* formulated by the philosopher, F. Jackson (1982). With the help of this thought experiment Jackson meant to stimulate discussions against a purely physicalist view of the universe, namely the suggestion that the universe, including mental processes, is entirely physical. This thought experiment tries to show that there are non-physical properties — and attainable knowledge — that can only be learned through conscious experience. Here is Frank Jackson's explanation:

Mary is a brilliant scientist who is, for whatever reason, forced to investigate the world from a black and white room via a black and white television monitor. She specialises in the neurophysiology of vision and acquires, let us suppose, all the physical information there is to obtain about what goes on when we see ripe tomatoes, or the sky, and use terms like "red" "blue" and so on. She discovers, for example, just which wavelength combinations from the sky stimulate the retina, and exactly how this produces via the central nervous system the contraction of the vocal cords and expulsion of air from the lungs that results in the uttering of the sentence "The sky is blue". What will happen when Mary is released from her black and white room or is given a colour television monitor? Will she learn anything or not? Put another way, Mary knows everything there is to know about colour except for one crucial thing: She's never actually experienced colour consciously. Her first experience of colour was something that she couldn't possibly have anticipated; there's a world of difference between academically knowing something versus having actual experience of that thing. This thought experiment teaches us that there will always be more to our perception of reality, including consciousness itself, than objective observation. It essentially shows us that we don't know what we don't know. This thought experiment also gives us hope for the future, should we augment our sensory capabilities and find ways to expand conscious awareness, we could open up entirely new avenues of psychological and subjective exploration.

L. Wittgenstein, in his book *Philosophical Investigations,* proposed a thought experiment that challenged the way we look at introspection and how it informs the language we use to describe sensations. For the thought experiment, Wittgenstein asks us to imagine a group of individuals, each of whom has a box containing something called a "beetle". No one can see into anyone else's box. Everyone is asked to describe their beetle — but each person only knows their own beetle. However, each person can only talk about their own beetle, as there might be different things in each person's box. Consequently, Wittgenstein says the subsequent descriptions cannot have a part in the "language game". Over time, people will talk about what is in their boxes, but the word "beetle" simply ends up meaning "that thing that is in a person's box". Why is this thought experiment disturbing? This mental experiment points out that the beetle is like our mind, and that we can't know exactly what it is like in another individual's mind. We can't know exactly what other people are experiencing, or the uniqueness of their perspective.

Suggested readings:

Jackson, F.: Epiphenomenal Qualia.In: *Philosophical Quarterly*, 1982, 32:27–36.
Parfit, D.: *Reasons and Persons.* Oxford: Clarendon Press, 1987.
Wilkes, K.: *Real People: Personal Identity without Thought Experiments.* Oxford: Oxford University Press, 1988.

VII Logical Fallacies

Keywords: slippery slope, straw man, fallacy, circularity, red herring

Fallacies are common errors in reasoning that will undermine the logic of any argument. Fallacies can be either illegitimate arguments or irrelevant points, and are often identified because they lack evidence that supports their claim. It is important both to avoid these common fallacies in your own arguments and watch for them in the arguments of others. The following text will illustrate only a small portion of the widespread types of fallacies.

Slippery slope. This is a conclusion based on the premise that if A happens, then eventually through a series of small steps, through B, C...X, Y, Z will happen too, basically equating A and Z. So, if we don't want Z to occur A must not be allowed to occur either. For example: If we ban Hummers because they are bad for the environment eventually the government will ban all cars, so we should not ban Hummers. In this example the author is equating banning Hummers with banning all cars, which is not the same thing.

Hasty Generalisation: This is a conclusion based on insufficient or biased evidence. In other words, you are rushing to a conclusion before you have all the relevant facts. For example: Even though it's only the first day, I can tell this is going to be a boring course. In this example, the author is basing their evaluation of the entire course on only one class, and on the first day which is notoriously boring and full of housekeeping tasks for most courses. To make a fair and reasonable evaluation the author must attend several classes, and possibly even examine the textbook, talk to the professor, or talk to others who have previously finished the course in order to have sufficient evidence on which to base their conclusion.

Post hoc ergo propter hoc: This is a conclusion that assumes that if "A" occurred after "B" then "B" must have caused "A". For example: I drank bottled water and now I am sick, so the water must have made me sick. In this example the author assumes that if one event chronologically follows another, the first event must have caused the second. But the illness could have been caused by the burrito the night before, a flu bug that had been working on the body for days, or a chemical spill across campus. There is no reason, without more evidence, to assume that the water caused the person to be sick.

Genetic Fallacy: This is a conclusion based on an argument that the origins of a person, idea, institute, or theory determine its character, nature, or worth. For example: The Volkswagen Beetle is an evil car because it was originally designed during Nazi era. In this example the author is equating the character of the car with the character of the people who built the car.

Begging the Claim: In this fallacy, the conclusion that the writer should prove is validated within the claim. For example: Filthy and polluting coal should be banned. Arguing that coal pollutes the earth and thus should be banned, would be logical. But the very conclusion that should be proved, that coal causes enough pollution to warrant banning its use, is already assumed in the claim by referring to it as "filthy and polluting".

Ignoratio elenchi (argument from ignorance): This fallacy restates the argument rather than actually proving it. These types of arguments are very common in philosophical writing and argumentation. Here is an example of a frequently used anti-materialist argument, the so called *argument from introspection*:

1. I can come to know about my mind (mental states) by introspection.

2. I cannot come to know about my brain (or any physical states) by introspection.

3. Therefore, my mind and my physical parts are distinct (by Leibniz's Law). I can know about my mind through looking into myself. I can know about my brain through external investigation.

A materialist has no problem with those two claims. But will a materialist admit the second premise? What if mental states are just brain states and we understand them in two different ways? It's like the same guy that Lois Lane knows through two ways of thinking about him – in one way, she thinks certain things about him (i.e., that he's a powerful hero with incredibly good vision), and in the other way she thinks different things about him (i.e., that he's a glasses-wearing reporter). He's the same guy. She just doesn't know it. So it would be if our brain is our mind. We can think of it in terms of beliefs, memories, and desires – from within. We can also think of it in terms of neurons, electrical signals, and gray matter – as if from an outside point of view. But maybe it's the same thing we're thinking about, just in two different ways. As before, a materialist might say our mind isn't just our brain, admitting that the conclusion is true, but still saying the mind isn't non-physical. If this is so, then the conclusion is true, but materialism is also true. Some materialists prefer to think of the mind as just the brain, and this move would be unattractive to them, which would require a more complex response.

Either/or: This is a conclusion that oversimplifies the argument by reducing it to only two sides or choices. For example: *We can either stop using cars or destroy the earth.* In this example, two choices are presented as the only options, yet the author ignores a range of other choices in between, such as developing cleaner technology, car sharing systems for necessities and emergencies, or better community planning to discourage daily driving.

Ad hominem: This is an attack on the character of a person, rather than their opinions or arguments. For example: Stating that someone's argument is incorrect because of her religious beliefs, such as, "Perhaps if you weren't part of the religious group that you are, you would see this quite differently." Disagreeing with an argument's or an author's conclusion, but accepting the reasons for believing the conclusion, is not an option in critical evaluation. If you disagree with a conclusion, then you must say so and explain why with an evaluation of the argument that allegedly supports it. Simply rejecting the position is not acceptable, nor are responses like, "Socrates can believe x because he is entitled to his opinion, but I disagree" or "I choose not to believe Russell" without any further explanation as to why. Evaluations of the author's historical, personal, or psychological background are not acceptable philosophical criticisms. "Anselm was biased because everyone in his time believed in God" or "Descartes believed what he was brought up to believe by the Jesuits" or "Aristotle was merely defending the interests of his privileged class" are not sufficient philosophical criticisms. In fact, these are fallacious ad hominem attacks on the person that ignore the merits of their arguments. Furthermore, stylistic evaluations of the author's work are not appropriate for philosophy papers. The purpose of a philosophical evaluation is not to comment on how clear or well-expressed the author's work is, nor is it to address whether or not the author has given enough examples. So comments like, "Sartre's argument is well put together" or "There are not enough examples" or "The argument is clearly stated and well-written" are not appropriate for a philosophy paper. Do not misrepresent the author's reasoning. If you are reconstructing someone else's argument, your evaluations will be stronger if you give the most charitable and accurate argument on their behalf that you can.

Ad populum: This is an emotional appeal that speaks to positive (such as patriotism, religion, democracy) or negative (such as terrorism or fascism) concepts, rather than the real issue at hand. For example: If you were a true Slovak you would support the rights of people to choose whatever vehicle they want. In this example, the author equates being a "true Slovak" – a concept that people want to be associated with, particularly in a time of war – with allowing people to buy any vehicle they want, even though there is no inherent connection between the two.

Petitio principii (circular reasoning, circular argument, begging the question): In general, this is the fallacy of assuming as a premise a statement that has the same meaning as the conclusion. One kind of *petitio prinicpii* is the use of an intermediate step in shifting to the same meaning from the premise to the conclusion. The link-ing of premises and conclusions return to the beginning, for example: "The soul is simple because it is immortal, and it must be immortal because it's simple". A good example of this type of argumentation is closely related to the problem of personal identity. Many people regard the idea that our persistence is intrinsically related to our psychology as obvious. The problem of cashing out this conviction in theoretical terms, however, is notoriously difficult. Psychological continuity relations are to be understood in terms of overlapping chains of direct psychological connections, that is, those causal and cognitive connections between beliefs, desires, intentions, experiential memories, character traits and so forth. This statement avoids two obvious problems.

Firstly, some attempts to cash out personal identity relations in psychological terms appeal exclusively to *direct* psychological connections. Such accounts face the problem that identity is a transitive relation while many psychological connections are not. Take memory as an example: suppose that Paul broke the neighbour's window as a kid, an incident he remembers vividly when he starts working as a primary school teacher in his late 20s. As an old man, Paul remembers his early years as a teacher, but has forgotten ever having broken the neighbour's window. Assume, for *reductio*, that personal identity consists in direct memory connections. In that case the kid is identical with the primary school teacher and the primary school teacher is identical with the old man; the old man, however, is not identical with the kid. Since this conclusion violates the transitivity of identity (which states that if an X is identical with a Y, and the Y is identical with a Z, then the X must be identical with the Z), personal identity relations cannot consist in direct memory connections. An appeal to overlapping layers or chains of psychological connections avoids the problem by permitting indirect relations: according to this view, the old man is identical with the kid precisely because they are related to each other by those causal and cognitive relations that connect kid and teacher and teacher and old man.

Secondly, memory alone is not necessary for personal identity, as a lack of memory through periods of sleep or coma do not obliterate one's survival of these states. An appeal to causal and cognitive connections which relate not only memory but other psychological aspects is sufficient to eradicate the problem. Let us say that we are dealing with psychological *connectedness* if the relations in question are direct causal or cognitive relations, and that we are dealing with psychological *continuity* if overlapping layers of psychological connections are appealed to (Parfit, 1987). One of the main problems a psychological approach faces is overcoming an alleged circularity associated with explicating personal identity relations in terms of psychological notions. Consider memory as an example. It seems that if John remembers having repaired the bike, then it is necessarily the case that John repaired the bike: saying that a person remembers having carried out an action which the person did not in fact carry out may be regarded as a misapplication of the verb "to remember". To be sure, one can remember *that* an action was carried out by somebody else; it seems to be a matter of necessity, however, that one can only have first-person memories of the experiences one had or the actions one carried out. Consequently, the objection goes, if memory and other psychological predicates are not impartial with regard to identity judgments, a theory that involves these predicates and that at the same time proposes to explicate such identity judgments is straightforwardly circular: it plainly assumes what it intends to prove.

To make things clearer, consider the case of *Teletransportation* above: if at t_2 Y on Mars remembers having had at t_1 X's experience on earth that the coffee is too hot, then, necessarily, X at t_1 is identical with Y at t_2. The dialectic of such thought experiments, however, requires that a description of the scenario is possible that does not presuppose the identity of the participants in question. We would wish to say that since X and Y share all psychological features, it is reasonable or intuitive to judge that X and Y are identical, and precisely *not* that since we describe the case as one in which there is a continuity between X's and Y's psychologies, X and Y are necessarily identical. If some psychological predicates presuppose personal identity in this way, an account of personal identity that constitutively appeals to such predicates is viciously circular.

Red Herring: This is a diversionary tactic that avoids the key issues, often by avoiding opposing arguments rather than addressing them. For example: The level of mercury in seafood may be unsafe, but what will fishers do to support their families? In this example the author switches the discussion away from the safety of the food and talks instead about an economic issue, the livelihood of those catching the fish. While one issue may affect the other, it does not mean we should ignore the possible safety issues because of the possible economic consequences to a few individuals.

An argument can be criticised if the reasons given in support of the conclusion are false. The argument for a conclusion succeeds or fails on the basis of the premises that support it. So if one or more of the premises are false, the conclusion will not follow. However, if you call the truth of the reasons into question, then you must provide your own reasons for doubting them. Simply expressing doubts or your own beliefs to the contrary without substantiation are of no real interest. It is very important to notice that when reasoning is given for a conclusion, then there is rarely any need to focus on the truth of the conclusion directly. The truth of the conclusion is a function of the truth of the reasons, and the degree of support the reasons give to the conclusion. Hence, whenever you call the truth of the conclusion into question, it should be either because you are questioning the truth of the reasons, or the degree of support the reasons give to the conclusion.

Another important basis for calling the truth of the reasons into question is logical consistency. Reasoning is logically inconsistent when it is committed to both the truth and the falsity of a certain statement. It is a basic law of logic that no statement can be both true and false, so anytime you find a contradiction you know that one of the things being claimed has to be false. As an example, consider this reasoning:

1. Addictive drugs take away a person's freedom.
2. Therefore, addictive drugs should not be legal.

As it stands, the argument seems to be committed to the truth of the general principle that it is wrong to take away a person's freedom. The problem is that making drugs illegal also takes away a person's freedom, specifically, the freedom to take drugs. Hence, the author is committed to a logical contradiction, that the statement, "It is wrong to take away a person's freedom" is both true and false.

An argument can be criticised because the reasons given don't support the conclusion. In some cases, the reasons offered in support for a conclusion may be true, but they still don't give us adequate grounds for accepting the conclusion. The simplest way to address this issue is to think in terms of producing counterexamples. A counterexample is an example that undermines the reasoning by showing that even if the reasons are true, they don't necessarily support the conclusion. Try to draft your own example!

Suggested readings:

Parfit, D.: *Reasons and Persons.* Oxford: Clarendon Press, 1987.
Wilkes, K.: *Real People: Personal Identity without Thought Experiments.* Oxford: Oxford University Press, 1988.
Wittgenstein, L.: *Philosophical Investigations.* Oxford: Blackwell, 1953.

Cognitive biases

Keywords: heuristics, automatisms, idols, overestimation, generalisation, supportive bias

As indicated in the previous chapter, clear and comprehensible writing requires clear and logical thinking. In reality, however, our minds are influenced by a variety of difficulties and confusions. In his work *New Organon* (1620) philosopher Francis Bacon has recognised negative aspects of *idols – errors* which repeatedly follow human mind in the process of knowledge. Bacon considered idols as false ideas declining reason from truth and better understanding of nature. According to Bacon, while some idols are inherent in human nature, others are acquired during lifetime. The first type is represented by *idols of the tribe* (idola tribus), for example, the habit of expecting more order in natural phenomena than is actually to be found. *Idols of the imprisoning cave* (idola specus) are based on personal prejudices, individual beliefs and passions. *Idols of the marketplace* (idola fori) are grounded in our trust to words that could lead to belief in nonexistent things. Bacon has considered this type of idols as the most dangerous. The last *idols of the theatre* (idoli theatri) express man's acceptance of ideas and beliefs without any sign of doubt or criticism.

Past decades of experimental research in cognitive psychology have profoundly supported Bacon's ideas on errors in cognition. Novel findings on the role and influence of cognitive biases on human thoughts and actions in various domains of society are linked up with the work of A. Tversky, P. Slovic and D. Kahneman. Laboratory experiments together with experimental research in real life conditions have demonstrated a number of common sources of biases, for example: a)framing, b) confirmation bias, c)overestimation, d)group conformity, e)sufficient agreement etc.

A *cognitive bias* is any of a wide range of observer effects identified in cognitive science and social psychology including very basic statistical, social attribution, and memory errors that are common to all human beings. Biases related to probability and decision making significantly affect the scientific method that is deliberately designed to minimise such bias from any one observer. Cognitive bias is considered as a distortion in the way we perceive reality. Many of these biases are often studied for how they affect business and economic situation. Exposure effect is a psychological artifact well known to advertisers: people express undue liking for things merely because they are familiar with them. Memory biases may either enhance or impair the recall of memory, or they may alter the content of what we report remembering.

Illusion of control is the tendency for human beings to believe they can control or at least influence outcomes that they demonstrably have no access to. In psychology and cognitive science, *confirmation bias* (or confirmatory bias) is a tendency to search for or interpret information in a way that does not contradict the previously held ideas and habits.

Self perception biases are the tendency to allow one's dispositions to affect one's way of interpreting information. Self perception biases are distortions of one's own view of self. The affectation or tendency to be ignorant of one's own biases is a case of the blind not knowing or ignoring that they are blind. This also includes viewing completed events as more predictable than they actually were.

Hindsight Bias can easily be observed outside the science building as Yorkies walking out of a math test will ask one another what they got on Option A and frustratedly proclaim they knew that was what they were supposed to do, but for some reason didn't apply it at the time.

Observer expectancy effect – known as the "observer effect" is a fallacy that can very easily skew results in qualitative scientific experimentation. It is the tendency to manipulate or misinterpret data so that it will support (or disprove) a hypothesis. Essentially, it is the tendency to see what you want or expect to see.

Framing Effect is the tendency to interpret information differently based on changes in context or description. A Yorkie might exhibit this in the stress they put on studying for a chemistry quiz in comparison to a chemistry test. Even though Ms. Trachsel will explain that test and quiz scores are valued equally, and this quiz will be the same length as an average test, you might still hear one Yorkie telling another that "It's just a quiz" implying that being a quiz makes it somehow less imperative or important, regardless of how many points it's worth.

Choice Supportive Bias – the propensity to believe your choices were better or more righteously chosen than they actually were. This tends to happen when an individual remembers only the positive aspects of the chosen option of a decision, and only the negative aspects of the rejected options. For example, a second semester senior who hasn't taken any AP classes might justify his choice by concentrating on how much stress he would have now had he taken any AP classes, while not thinking about the benefits of passing the AP test and potentially getting college credit. Cognitive biases in logic and decisions are shown mostly through how people go about solving problems in different ways, make various choices, and judge different situations.

Base rate fallacy is the inclination for someone to base his judgements on specifics rather than the big picture. An example of this could be a York Senior who chooses a college for having a strong chemistry program and ignores other aspects such as its location in the middle of a desert. Rather frequent is also *the zero-risk bias* – the tendency for someone to try to eliminate a small risk rather than lower the likeliness of a great risk. An example of this could be a Yorkie that decides against joining the cross country team because they run on trails adjacent to areas that could contain unexploded ordinance. Rather than always choosing public transportation over driving a car to greatly reduce the risk of death in a transportation accident, the Yorkie reduces a small chance of getting blown to bits. This bias stems from a desire to reduce risk based on proportion rather than by chance.

Anchoring means the inclination for someone to allow one piece of information to outweigh others when making a decision. An example might be a couple considering the fact that the girl they hired to babysit their children goes to Stanford to be more important than the side facts that that girl skips half her classes, rides a motorcycle and brings her boyfriend with her to babysitting jobs.

Belief Bias – the tendency for someone to ignore logical error in an argument based on how believable a conclusion may be. For instance, people often buy into weight loss commercials that promise you could lose 20 pounds despite the illogical claim that you don't have to diet and only have to use their method for ten minutes every day for two weeks.

*Semmelweis reflex*is known as the reflex like tendency to ignore or reject any contradictory information against what one already believes. An example might be someone who does not believe that high fructose corn syrup is right for their children after being told it was unhealthy, despite solid research and facts disputing that misconception.

A probability bias arises when someone misinterprets precedents or past information and acts on this inaccuracy. Dangerous is also gambler's *fallacy*, the propensity to believe that happenings of the past determine what will happen in the future. Just as its name predicts, this is most commonly exemplified by gamblers whom mistakenly tend to think along the lines that since they lost their game the last six times, they have a much greater chance of winning this time, or the next time, or the time after that. Predictive biases are most usually related to someone holding the inaccurate belief that they prematurely know information about events or people based on large or general ideas rather than specifics.

Conformity biases are the most socially based cognitive biases that are exemplified by people young and old in instances varying from politics to surfing.

In the book, *The Illusion of Conscious Will* (2002), psychologist D. Wegner has finessed all the usual arguments in a remarkable demonstration that psychology can sometimes transform philosophy. Instead of struggling with the usual debates about the compatibility of determinism and free will, Wegner shows how the *feeling* of willing arises. This means that we might at last understand why "all experience is for it" without having to invoke the real thing. The feeling of willing, says Wegner, arises because we have to decide whether actions are caused by ourselves or by other people. This decision depends on three principles: priority, consistency, and exclusivity. Put simply, if our thoughts come *before* an action, are compatible with that action, and there are no other likely causes, then we conclude that we did it, and we get the feeling of conscious will.

Many ingenious experiments provide evidence for Wegner's theory. The spiritualists' Ouija board might seem a strange choice, but lends itself well to investigating the feeling of control. In a classic Ouija session, people sit around a table with their forefingers on a upturned glass or a little wheeled board which, without them deliberately pushing, soon begins to move about and point to letters placed in a circle around it. In Wegner's modern version a small board is fixed to a computer mouse. Wearing headphones, his two participants hear the names of objects while letting the mouse roam freely over an "I-Spy" board covered with little pictures. They then stop the mouse on any picture they like. The first participant is asked to rate how strongly she felt that she chose the stopping place herself. Unbeknown to her, the other person is a confederate and, on some trials, forces the mouse to a particular picture. Even on these occasions the proband is often convinced that she willed the choice herself. Further experiments confirm Wegner's *priority principle* – that the stopping place is experienced as "willed" when the picture name is heard just before the stop.

In the traditional Ouija board, the messages are supposedly from spirits of the dead but, as was showed in 1853, the pointer is actually moved by unconscious muscular action, or ideomotor influence. Wegner reviews the evidence for ideomotor effects, and it is most refreshing, in a 21st century book, not only to find the early studies are not ignored, but to read such a thorough and engaging review of them. When, for example, Wegner asked people not to think of a white bear, they were plagued by thoughts of white bears, but the same effect can happen with actions. This can explain that peculiar conviction I sometimes have that I might do something terrible, like throwing myself under a train. Once the dangerous thought comes up I try to suppress it, which makes me think about it more. Then, by ideomotor action, I am more likely actually to do it. So I do not, after all, have some repressed death wish or dire mental sickness. It is just the feeling of willing. By the illusion of conscious will Wegner does not mean to reject the very existence of the feeling, but the false idea that our *conscious thoughts* cause our actions. This is caused by the simple mistake of confusing correlation with causality. When we decide to do something, we are first aware of our conscious thoughts about the action, then we observe the action happening, and finally we conclude that our thoughts *caused* the action. In fact, says Wegner, unconscious processes caused both the conscious thoughts and the action.

Suggested readings:

Bacon, F.: *The New Organon.* Jardine, L., Silverthorne, M.(Eds.), Cambridge Texts in the History of Philosophy, 2000.

Kahneman, D., Slovic, P.,Tversky, A.: *Judgment under uncertainty: Heuristics and biases.* Cambridge: Cambridge University Press, 1982.

Wegner, D.: *The Illusion of Conscious Will.* Cambridge: MIT Press, 2002.

Bibliography

Aristotle: *On Rhetoric: A Theory of Civic Discourse*. 2nd ed. Trans. George A. Kennedy. New York: Oxford UP, 2007.

Burke, K.:*A Rhetoric of Motives*. Berkeley: University of California Press, 1969.

Bacon, F.: *The New Organon*. Jardine, L., Silverthorne, M.(Eds.),Cambridge Texts in the History of Philosophy, 2000.

Blackmore, S.: Consciousness: An Introduction. London: Oxford University Press, 2011.

Block, N., Flanagan, O, Guzeldere, G.: *The Nature of Consciousness: Philosophical and Scientific Debates,* Cambridge: MIT Press, 1996.

Chalmers, D.: *The Conscious Mind*. New York: Oxford University Press, 1996.

Damasio, A. R.: *Descartes error: Emotion, reason, and the human brain.* New York: Penguin Books, 1994.

Dennett, D.: Consciousness Explained. Boston: Little, Brown, 1991.

Dennett, D.: Freedom Evolves. London: Allen Lane, 2003.

Richard, J., Paine, Ch.: *Writing Today*. New York: Pearson Education, 2010.

Davidson, D.: Mentálne udalosti. In: *Čin, myseľ, jazyk*. Bratislava: Archa, 1997.

Eysenk, M., Keane, M.: *Kognitivní psychologie*. Praha: Academia, 2008.

Churchland, P. S.: *Brain-Wise: Studies in Neurophilosophy*. Cambridge: The MIT Press, 2002.

Churchland, P. M.: Matter and Consciousness. Cambridge: MIT Press, 1999.

Churchland, P. M.: The Engine of Reason, the Seat of the Soul: A Philosophical Journey into the Brain. Cambridge: MIT Press, 1995.

Fodor, J.:*The Modularity of Mind: An Essay on Faculty Psychology.* Cambridge: MIT Press, 1983.

Jackson, F.: Epiphenomenal Qualia. In: *Philosophical Quarterly*, 1982, 32:27–36.

Gazanniga, M., Ivry, R., Mangun, G.: *Cognitive Neuroscience: The Biology of the Mind*. New York: W.W. Norton, 2002.

Kahneman, D., Slovic, P.,Tversky, A.: *Judgment under uncertainty: Heuristics and biases*. Cambridge: Cambridge University Press, 1982.

Lakoff, G., Johnson, M.: *Philosophy in the Flesh*. New York: Basic Books, 1999.

Locke, J.: *An Essay Concerning Human Understanding*. New York: Prometheus Books, 1995.

Markram, H.: The Blue Brain Project. In: *Nature Reviews Neuroscience*, 2006, 7(2):153–60.

Martinich, A. P.: *Philosophical Writing: An Introduction*. Oxford: Blackwell Publishing, 2005.

Murray, D. M.: Teach Writing as a Process Not Product. In: Villanueva, V. (ed.): *Cross-Talk in Comp Theory: A Reader*. Urbana, NCTE 2003, 3–6.

Parfit, D.: *Reasons and Persons*, Oxford: Clarendon Press, 1987.

Raimes, A.: *Pocket keys for writers*, 3rd Edition. New York: Wadsworth Cengage Learning, 2010.

Sacks, O.: *Muž, který si pletl manželku s kloboukem*. Praha: Mladá fronta, 1993.

Sternberg, R.J.: *Kognitivní psychologie*. Praha: Portál, 2002.

Swales, J. M., C. B. Feak: *Academic writing for graduate students: Essential tasks and skills*, 2nd Edition. Ann Arbor: University of Michigan Press, 2009.

Wegner, D.: *The Illusion of Conscious Will*. Cambridge: MIT Press, 2002.

Wilkes, K.: *Real People: Personal Identity without Thought Experiments*. Oxford: Oxford University Press, 1988.

Wittgenstein, L.: *Philosophical Investigations*. Oxford: Blackwell, 1953.

Whorf, B., John B. Carroll (ed.):*Language, Thought, and Reality: Selected Writings of Benjamin Lee Whorf*. Cambridge: MIT Press, 1956.

Silvia Gáliková, born in 1962 in Bratislava has graduated at the Faculty of Philosophy, University of P.J. Šafárik in Prešov in 1988. She continued her post-graduate study at the Institute of Philosophy at Slovak Academy Of Sciences in Bratislava. S. Gáliková concentrates her research on contemporary philosophy of mind. Her teaching includes courses on philosophy of mind and conscious-ness, selected topics in the history of philosophy and cognitive science. Since 2008 she is a lecturer and tutor at the Deaprtment of Philosophy, Faculty of Philosophy at Trnava University in Trnava and author of Introduction to the philosophy of mind (2001), Psyché (2007), Mind in science (2013).

Európska únia
Európsky sociálny fond

Európska únia

Operačný program
VZDELÁVANIE

VÝSKUMNÁ
AGENTÚRA